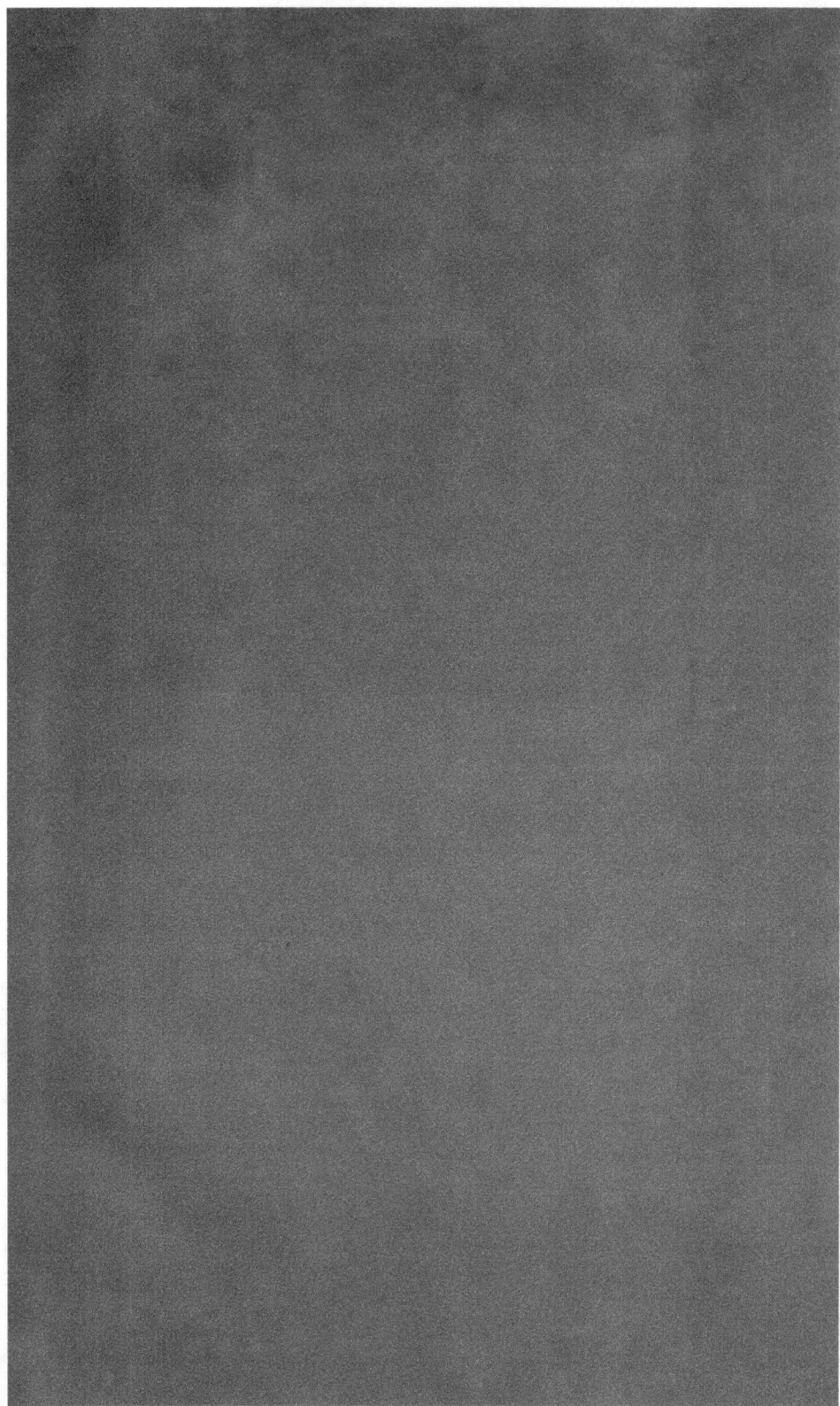

Asia's Appeal to America

(REVISED EDITION)

An Address

by

Sidney L. Gulick

Secretary of the Commission on International
Justice and Goodwill of the Federal Council of
the Churches of Christ in America

Secretary of the American Council of the World
Alliance for the Promotion of International
Friendship through the Churches

105 East Twenty-Second Street
New York City

105 East Twenty-Second Street
New York City

ASIA'S APPEAL TO AMERICA.

Europe's catastrophe has suddenly shown how closely interwoven is the fabric of the modern world. The interlinking of the life and interests of the nations had advanced much further than was realized Even Asia begins to figure as a mighty factor in occidental affairs. Some regard it as ominous. We talk of the "yellow peril;" yet for decades, nay for centuries, Asiatics have resented an actual and progressively overwhelming "white peril."

On the one hand there is China. Not for a century has her outlook been so bright. An alien dynasty has been driven from the throne; the nation is pushing forward with remarkable insistence for modern forms of government; the opium curse has been substantially eradicated; vigorous efforts are being made to eliminate political graft; financial solvency seems now assured; occidental education is proceeding rapidly in many centers; and desire for reforms is widespread. If China can avoid further alien intrusion her future is decidedly hopeful. We may not, however, forget that China faces many serious problems. Her internal political problems are by no means settled. Complete stability and order are still to be achieved. Reactionary forces will offer serious obstacles. The traditions, ignorance and inertia of her masses cannot fail to delay her development. These, however, are considerations that should call for sympathetic help rather than for pessimistic criticism.

And there is Japan. Her heroic struggles to meet the new world-situation that confronted her when she came out of her long isolation called forth deep admiration in America. The brilliant ability of her students and national leaders and the whole-souled patriotism of her people have received full recognition and evoked high praise. Japan, however, has reached so high a development of power and ambition that some begin to fear and suspect her.

1

A NEW ERA IN HUMAN HISTORY.

The adoption by Japan and China of the mechanical, economic, social and political elements of occidental civilization constitutes the beginning of a new era in human history. The changes rapidly occurring in Asia demand our attention. At this juncture, therefore, it is well that we pause to consider the entire situation. What is the duty of America at this time in its relations to Asia? What responsibilities have we, if any? and, what is even more pertinent, what may we do to put and keep ourselves right with the Orient?

Both China and Japan are facing mighty problems. The early solution of those problems concerns, not themselves alone, but all the world. Our fate is in truth involved in theirs. The urgency accordingly of their appeal should command our earnest and sympathetic attention and secure our action. Our own national welfare through the long future, no less than our national character, are intimately involved in our response to that appeal.

China's appeal for justice and friendly treatment was made decades ago, but has been completely ignored by the statesmen and Christians of America. Japan's appeal is more recent. Will America heed it any better?

AMERICAN TREATMENT OF CHINA.

The story of our dealings with China is as a whole one of which we need not be ashamed. We have not seized her territory, bombarded her ports, extracted indemnities or pillaged her. capitals as have other nations. On the contrary, we have helped preserve her from "partition" at a grave crisis in her relations with western lands. We returned a considerable part of her Boxer indemnity that came to us. We have stood for the open door and a square deal. Our consular courts have been models of probity and justice. The work of our missionaries in hospitals, education,

2

and in famine and flood relief has been highly appreciated.

In consequence of such factors the Chinese as a nation hold today a highly gratifying attitude of friendship toward us. So conspicuous has this friendship and preferential treatment become since the establishment of the Republic that other nations have begun to note it. In the reforms taking place in China, especially in her educational system, in her political and social reorganization, and in her moral and religious awakening, the influence of Americans is far beyond that exercised by any other people.

When we turn, however, to the story of what many Chinese have suffered here, our cheeks tingle with shame. The story would be incredible were it not overwhelmingly verified by ample documentary evidence. Treaties have pledged rights, immunities and protection. They have, nevertheless, been disregarded and even knowingly invaded; and this not only by private individuals, but by legislators, and administrative officials. Scores of Chinese have been murdered, hundreds wounded and thousands robbed by anti-Asiatic mobs, with no protection for the victims or punishment for the culprits. State legislatures, and even Congress, have enacted laws in contravention of treaty provisions. Men appointed to federal executive offices have at times administered those laws and regulations in offensive methods.

Let us consider briefly some of the details of the situation. It will be well to premise that all in all Chinese in America have not been treated badly. In general they have received police protection; their lives have been safe; they have been able to carry on successful business. So attractive to them is the opportunity of life here that they have stayed on and every year not a few succeed in smuggling their way into our land. The dark picture about to be sketched, accordingly, is not to be understood as describing the regular features of Chinese experience.

AMERICAN CHINESE TREATY PLEDGES.

Adequately to appreciate the full significance of our anti-Chinese legislation we must begin the story with a few quotations from treaties by which America invited Chinese to this country.

Article V. of the treaty of 1868 reads in part:

"The United States of America and the Emperor of China cordially recognize the inherent and inalienable right of man to change his home and allegiance and also the mutual advantage of the free migration and emigration of their citizens and subjects respectively . . . for purposes of curiosity, trade or as permanent residents."

But Article VI, after promising reciprocal "most favored nation" enjoyment of "privileges, immunities and exemptions," adds that this does not "confer naturalization" upon their respective citizens. This clause doubtless meant that the mere fact of residence in the other's land did not of itself alone carry citizenship in that land. For up till 1880 a few Chinese were granted naturalization in the United States. In harmony with the provisions of this treaty considerable Chinese immigration into the United States occurred during the seventh and eighth decades of the last century.

Anti-Chinese agitation soon developed in the Pacific Coast states. Growing violent in the seventies, it led to the sending of a Commission to China which negotiated the supplementary treaty of 1880.

The principal provisions of this treaty are as follows:

Article I provides that "the Government of the United States may regulate, limit or suspend such coming or residence of Chinese (laborers), but may not absolutely prohibit it. The limitation or suspension shall be reasonable and shall apply only to . . . laborers."

Article II provides that: "Chinese laborers who are now in the United States shall be allowed to go and come of their own free will and accord, and shall be

4

accorded all the rights, privileges, immunities, and exemptions which are accorded to citizens and subjects of the most favored nation."

Article III provides that in case of ill treatment the "Government of the United States will exert all its power to devise measures for their protection and to secure to them the same rights, privileges, immunities and exemptions as may be enjoyed by citizens or subjects of the most favored nation, and to which they are entitled by treaty."

Article IV provides that legislative measures dealing with Chinese shall be "communicated to the Government of China," and if found "to work hardship upon the subjects of China, consultations shall be held to the end that mutual and unqualified benefit may result."

DISREGARD OF TREATY PLEDGES.

In spite, however, of the complete cessation of Chinese labor immigration, and in spite of the promises of our Government to provide protection, "and most favored nation treatment," the unjust treatment of Chinese did not cease. The outrages committed on the Chinese during the eighties were even more frightful and inexcusable than those of the preceding decade.

In his discussion of the question whether the Federal Government should protect aliens in their treaty rights, Ex-President William H. Taft, cites the cases of fifty Chinamen who suffered death at the hands of American mobs in our Western States, and of one hundred and twenty others, many of whom were wounded and robbed of all their property. The list does not profess to be complete. All these outrages have occurred since 1885.

"In an official note of February 15, 1886, riots were reported at Bloomfield, Redding, Boulder Creek, Eureka and other towns in California, involving murder, arson and robbery, and it was added that thousands of Chinese had been driven from their homes."

5

None of the criminals were punished in spite of the article in the treaty which expressly provides that in case "Chinese laborers meet with ill treatment at the hands of other persons, the Government of the United States will exert all its power to devise measures for their protection and secure to them the same rights, privileges, immunities, and exemptions as may be enjoyed by citizens or subjects of the most favored nation and to which they are entitled by treaty." Congress, it is true, has voted indemnities for families of those murdered, but financial remuneration can hardly be supposed to take the place of justice or to be a substitute for observance of treaty pledges.

It is sometimes said that Italians and other aliens suffered similarly from mob violence and they too were not protected, nor were the criminals punished, and that therefore China cannot complain of exceptional treatment. But is it not obvious that failure of the United States to fulfill its treaty pledges to Italy and other countries in no wise justifies similar failure toward China? Does it not rather show that the United States is culpable for failure to make adequate provision for the faithful performance of its treaty pledges? This moral and legal defect has become most conspicuous in our relations with China, but its culpability is in no wise lessened—rather it is aggravated—as soon as it becomes clear that the defect is entirely due to the failure of Congress to take the needed action. For provision for such action is made by the Constitution of the United States.

ANTI- CHINESE LEGISLATION.

The failure of Congress seems inexcusable, for it found time to enact not only the first general exclusion law in harmony with the treaty with China, but also several supplementary laws, of which important clauses are admittedly in contravention to the treaty.

The Scott Law of 1888 and the Geary Law of 1892 are still in force, though the essential injustice of some of their provisions and their disregard of Chinese

6

treaty rights are now recognized. They are producing constant anti-American feeling among Chinese legitimately in America. Even in cosmopolitan New York and in Boston, Chinese sometimes suffer from the acts of federal officers who supervise Chinese residents in the United States, acts, moveover which are required by the laws and administrative regulations dealing with the Chinese.

With regard to the Scott Law, Senator Sherman said that it was "one of the most vicious laws that have passed in my time in Congress." It was passed as a "mere political race between the two houses . . . in the face of a Presidential election." Senator Dawes sarcastically referred to keeping the treaties as long as we had a mind to. The law was "a rank unblushing repudiation of every treaty obligation . . . unwarranted by any existing danger—a violation such as the United States would not dare to commit toward any warlike nation of Europe."

With regard to the Geary Law, Professor Coolidge makes the following statement:

"Meanwhile the Chinese Minister at Washington, the Consul-General at San Francisco and the Yamen at Peking were also protesting against the act. The Chinese Minister had steadily protested ever since the Scott Act against the plain violation of treaty; just preceeding the Geary Act, he wrote six letters to Mr. Blaine only two of which were so much as acknowledged. He now declared that the Geary Act was worse than the Scott Act, for it not only violated every single article of the treaty of 1880 but also denied bail, required white witnesses, allowed arrest without warrant and put the burden of proof on the Chinese. He quoted our own statement on the harsh and hasty character of the act, not required by any existing emergency, whose political motive was well understood both in China and the United States. In his final protest he said: 'The statute of 1892 is a violation of every principle of justice, equity, reason and fairdealing between two friendly powers.'"

THE SUPREME COURT.

Not unnaturally, both the Chinese, and Americans interested in maintaining right relations with China, looked to the Supreme Court to declare unconstitutional such laws as contravene treaties—for are not treaties "the supreme law of the land"? The Chinese accordingly brought forward a test case dealing with certain provisions of the Scott Act (1888).

Judge Field, who pronounced the judgment of the court, said: "It must be conceded that the Act of 1888 is in contravention of the treaty of 1868 and of the supplemental treaty of 1880, but it is not on that account invalid. . . . It (a treaty) can be deemed . . . only the equivalent of a legislative act, to be repealed or modified at the pleasure of Congress. . . . It is the last expression of sovereign will and must control." "The question whether our government was justified in disregarding its engagements with another nation is not one for the determination of the courts. . . . This court is not a censor of the morals of the other departments of the government."

This made it clear that a treaty is not the "supreme law of the land" except as Congress makes it so. Congress can, without violation of the Constitution, repeal or amend any part of a treaty even without securing the consent of the other party to the treaty, and even without conference. Treaties are declared by this decision to have no binding power upon Congress. The Supreme Court declined to take note of the moral obligations of treaty pledges. Disappointing though it may be, this is unquestionably correct law. Aliens deprived by Congress of rights promised by treaties may not appeal to the Supreme Court for the enforcement of those rights. The Administration can indeed use the entire military force of the country to make a foreign nation observe its treaty obligations to us, but

8

according to the interpretation of our Constitution, neither the Administration nor the Supreme Court can hold Congress to the observance of our treaty pledges. The President has of course the power to veto an act of Congress, but experience shows that even Presidents do not always regard treaties as binding, for the treaty-ignoring laws have been signed by the Presidents then in office. This makes it clear that the moral obligations of our nation must be carefully safeguarded by the people themselves. We must hold our representatives in Congress to their moral responsibilities in international as in all other relations. This is a matter of moral energy——not of law.

AN OMINOUS SITUATION.

Dr. Bernhard Dernberg, defending Germany's invasion of Belgium on the ground of necessity, argues that the United States takes the same attitude toward treaties as does Germany, and cites this very decision of the Supreme Court rendered by Judge Field. If we maintain that the United States was justified in its disregard of our treaty with China, what right have we to condemn Germany for its diregard of its treaty with Belgium? The degree of the consequences indeed differ enormously, but are not the moral issues identical?

CONGRESS CONTRAVENES TREATIES.

In 1904 Congress again contravened the treaty with China. The treaty (1880) states that "The United States may regulate, limit, or suspend such coming or residence (of Chinese labor immigration) but may not absolutely prohibit it. The limitation or suspension shall be reasonable."

In harmony with these explicit provisions, Congress provided in 1882, in 1892 and again in 1902 for the temporary suspension of Chinese labor immigration for periods of ten years each. By 1894, however, so many of the laws and treasury regulations dealing with the Chinese had become so manifestly violations of the treaty that a new one was prepared in Washington to meet the difficulty, embodying the principle features of the anti-Chinese legislation. It proved, however, so obnoxious to the Chinese Government that at the first opportunity, namely at the expiration (1904) of the ten-year period for which the treaty itself provided, China denounced the treaty. The relations of the two countries therefore fell back onto the treaty of 1880, which had been neither rejected nor amended. In spite, however, of its provisions quoted above, Congress then enacted that "all laws regulating, suspending or prohibiting the coming of Chinese persons—are hereby reenacted, extended and continued without modification, limitation or condition", thus again plainly contravening the treaty.

THE FOOTBALL OF PARTY POLITICS.

The history of anti-Chinese legislation, as it has been carried through Congress under the pressure of legislators from the Pacific Coast states, from the eighth decade of the last century even down to the present, and the way in which the Asiatic problem has been made the "football of party politics" are ill omens for the future relations of America with the Orient. Eight times in fourteen years anti-Chinese agitation on the Pacific Coast secured increasingly drastic and obnoxious legislation in Congress. "All but one of these measures was passed on the eve of an election under political pressure for avowed political purposes." That legislation contravened plain provisions of the treaties, to say nothing of the spirit, and disregarded courteous protests of Chinese ministers and ambassadors. China sent in a "stream of dignified and ineffectual protests". The Chinese Minister even charged us with duplicity in negotiating the treaty of 1880. "Mr. Bayard assured him that the President would veto any legislation which might be passed in violation of the treaty."

If the faithful observance of treaties between the nations of Europe constitutes the very foundation of

10

civilization, as we are now vehemently told—and this is said to be the real reason why Great Britain is in the war—is not the faithful observance of treaties with Asiatics the foundation of right relations with them? In other words, do not treaties ratified by Congress have moral aspects which should place them on a higher level of authority than the ordinary acts of Congress? Disregard by Congress of this fundamental principle for the maintenance of right international relations is fraught with ominous consequences. Congress of course has the right to abrogate a treaty, but there is a right way and also a wrong way to do it. Is it any more right for a nation to abrogate an inconvenient treaty by simply passing laws in contravention to certain of its pledges than it is for an individual who has made a promise to another individual giving *quid pro quo* suddenly and without conference to ignore that promise? Is it conceivable that Congress would have treated China as it has, had she been equipped as Japan is today, with the instruments of occidental civilization?

Now when China becomes equipped with a daily press and adequate world news, when her national organization becomes better unified, more efficient and better equipped, when her self-consciousness is more perfectly developed, and when she learns that Chinese entering America have often suffered ignominious treatment, that Chinese lawfully here are deprived of rights guaranteed by long standing treaties, and that privileges granted as a matter of course to individuals of other nations are refused to Chinese on exclusively racial grounds, is it not as certain as the sunrise that Chinese friendship for America will wane and serious possibilities develop?

Although China's appeal to us comes along many other lines also, I shall not dwell upon them. It is enough for the moment to note that there are such.

Let us turn next to American-Japanese relations.

11

AMERICAN TREATMENT OF JAPAN.

For half a century that treatment was above reproach, and, being in marked contrast to that of other lands, called forth a gratitude toward, friendship for, and confidence in, America that Americans cannot easily realize. I must not do more than refer to our helpful diplomacy and our welcome to her students, giving them every facility, not only in our schools and colleges, but in our factories and industries.

The mutual attitude, however, of our two countries has begun to change. Tension more or less exists between us today. Papers in both countries frequently assert in startling headlines that war is certain. Multitudes in both lands accept these statements without question, and are developing mutual suspicion, distrust, and animosity. False stories are widely circulated in each land about the other, which are readily believed.

What is the cause of the new situation? And what should we do to remedy it? Let us briefly study Japan's problem.

Japan first came in contact with the white nations of Europe about 1650. For sixty years they had free opportunity. Under the instruction of Roman Catholic missionaries, many hundred thousand Japanese became Christians. Then Japan took fright at the white man's methods and ambitions. She closed her doors, drove out the missionaries and merchants, exterminated the Christian religion, and till 1853 lived a life of almost complete national seclusion. No Japanese were allowed to go abroad nor were foreigners allowed to enter her land.

THE WHITE PERIL

All this was done to escape the occidental flood, which, during the intervening three hundred years, has engulfed the peoples of North, Central and South America, and large parts of Africa, Asia and Australia. China was forced by the so-called opium wars to give

to white peoples, not only privileges for the abomin-
able opium trade, but possession of ports for military
and naval bases. Japan, unable longer to resist the en-
croachment of foreigners, in 1854 made treaties. After
nearly a score of years of inner turmoil and a revolu-
tion, she frankly accepted the new world-situation cre-
ated by the white nations, and undertook to learn their
methods in order to meet them on a basis of equality.
She has learned and is now equipped with "civilization," with bayonets, bullets and battleships.

RENEWED AGGRESSIONS IN CHINA.

In the nineties, the "powers" of Europe, having com-
pleted their "division of Africa," began to look with
greedy eyes on China. In 1896, Germany, Russia and
France compelled Japan to return Port Arthur to
China in order to maintain, as they stated in their de-
ceitful diplomacy, the integrity of China, and provide
for the permanent peace of the Far East. Then in
1897-1898, Germany took Kiao-Chao as indemnity for
the killing of two German missionaries. Russia took
Port Arthur to keep up the balance, England took
Wei-hai-wei and France, Kwanchau. In each case,
the impotent Manchu Government made treaties with
the aggressive "friendly powers," giving them increasing concessions and privileges. But the people got
anxious. These occidental aggressions led (1900) to
the "Boxer Uprising." China's common people sought
to turn the white man out and keep "China for the
Chinese."

But it was too late. Six "civilized" armies marched
up to Peking, and, to teach China a lesson regarding
the sacredness of treaties and the white man's "rights,"
they saddled upon China an indemnity of 450,000,000
taels which at the protocol rate of exchange equals
$332,900,000, far exceeding the actual costs. Poor
China!

Then, according to mutual agreement, all the allies
withdrew their troops stationed in and around Peking.
Difficulties soon began, however, to develop with re-

13

gard to the situation in Manchuria and Korea. Russia, ignoring her promise of April, 1902, to withdraw her troops from Manchuria, began instead to send in thousands more.' Japan got anxious. Negotiations between Russia and Japan were slow and fruitless. Russia dallied and delayed, meanwhile increasing her forces, completing her Siberian railroad, and gaining diplomatic and other footholds in Korea. That policy produced the war with Japan.

THE RUSSO-JAPANESE WAR

Japan felt that the complete possession by Russia of Manchuria, Mongolia and Korea threatened her very existence as an independent nation. The "partition of China" also, she felt, would be a mere question of time. But Japan's earnest grasp at "civilization" had been so far successful that single-handed, though indirectly supported by her alliance with Great Britain, she beat back the bear from the north, and for the time being saved, not only herself, but also China from the further encroachments of the nations of Europe, and from that increasing white supremacy that had swept over all of South Asia from Messopotamia to Cochin China and in North Asia from European Russia to Alaska. In the meantime, however, Japan's own problems were deepening.

JAPAN'S PLIGHT

Her population of 50,000,000, living on islands of less than 140,000 square miles (357 to the square mile), is growing at the rate of 700,000 annually. (California, with a population of 2,500,000, possesses 160,000 square miles. England's population is 356, while China proper averages less than 250 to the square mile.) Japan's mountainous islands are not naturally fertile nor possessed of any considerable mineral resources. Japanese emigration to America, Canada, New Zealand, Australia or Africa, all sparsely peopled and possessed of vast natural resources, has become impossible because these lands are held by white nations and are declared to be "white man's lands." Japan's debt of

14

over $1,000,000,000 was incurred in resisting the "white peril," and her annual expense for army and navy with which to protect herself from the aggressive peoples of Europe is $160,000,000 annually. Japan's aggregate national wealth is only about $30,000,000,000, while that of Great Britain is placed at some $80,-000,000 and that of the United States at $187,000,-000. Such is a bare outline of Japan's plight.

In the course of the history sketched above, Japanese laborers were invited first to Hawaii and later to California. At first they were welcomed. But with increasing numbers in California difficulties developed. In 1907 the situation became so acute that Japan, fearing the consequences and desiring by every honorable means to retain America's friendship and show her gratitude, entered upon the "Gentlemen's Agreement," by which no additional Japanese labor immigration to the United States should be allowed.

For eight years that agreement has been strictly carried out, resulting in a diminution of Japanese laborers in America of several thousand.

In spite, however, of these mutually honorable and friendly relations of the two governments, the anti-Japanese agitation continued in California and resulted in 1913 in anti-Japanese legislation.

It was highly resented by Japan as an affront to her national honor. It could hardly have been viewed otherwise for Japan was honorably fulfilling her agreement. Japanese in California were diminishing in number and the amount of land owned by Japanese was a paltry 13,000 acres.

JAPAN'S CONTENTION.

It needs to be clearly understood that Japan is not asking for special privilege of any kind; not even for free opportunity for immigration.

The sole point of Japan's contention with America is, that **Japanese already in America shall not be subjected to differential race legislation, which is naturally** regarded as humiliating and unfriendly. There is no immigration question. It is a question of national honor. But Americans should not forget that in spite of recent rebuff, anti-Asiatic legislation, unkind words, a suspicious attitude, and unfriendly treatment, there has been in Japan a remarkable spirit of patience and moderation.

Japan is still hoping that some method will be found of providing for California's just demands without subjecting her to humiliation. She has taken at its face value the first treaty she ever made with a white race, namely, with America, which reads: "There shall be perfect, permanent and universal peace and sincere and cordial amity between the United States and Japan and between their people respectively, without exception of persons and places." This friendship, solemnly pledged, has been loyally maintained by Japan. But it cannot be denied that her friendly feelings and her admiration for America have considerably cooled. Many indeed are indignant; all are waiting eagerly to learn if America as a whole will support the anti-Asiatic policy so urgently pressed by Pacific Coast agitators. Indefinite continuation, however, of Japanese patience under treatment regarded as humiliating is not to be assumed.

Japan stands for national dignity and honor in international relations. She asks for full recognition among the nations. For this she has been strenuously striving for half a century. Is she not to be respected for it? Is not this sensitiveness and insistence one of the evidences that she deserves it? Economic opportunity in California is not the point of her interest or insistence, but recognition of manhood equality. Is not the honor of a nation of more importance than everything else? Is the maintenance of friendship possible between two nations when one insists on treatment or legislation that humiliates the other?

If now America desires to maintain the historic friendship with Japan and do her justice, we must first of all understand the real point of her contention. We must look at the questions involved from the standpoint not only of our interests but also of hers; we must gain her viewpoint, appreciate her problems, sympathize with her efforts, and recognize her attainments.

Such in bare outlines are a few of the multiform appeals to America of China and Japan. In the briefest term we may say that they seek for just and courteous treatment at our hands. They are not demanding economic advantages or opportunity, but human justice; respect for them as men.

How will America meet this appeal? Shall we go on our way unheeding? Shall we continue to disregard our treaties and humiliate our mighty neighbors across the Pacific? That were an ominous course.

Has not the time come for America to revise her Oriental policy? Can we not find a method for safeguarding our own welfare in ways that will neither humiliate them nor do them injustice?

HOW SHOULD AMERICA RESPOND?

First of all, Americans must be informed. A campaign of education in regard to Asiatic relations is urgently needed.

In the second place, we need a new Oriental policy. Such a policy would seem to require:

1. Congressional legislation giving adequate responsibility and authority to the Federal administration for the care and protection of aliens.

2. Immigration and other laws that treat all races exactly alike—this, and this alone, is friendly.

3. The law, moreover, should admit only so many immigrants as we can Americanize. This preserves our institutions and prevents economic disturbance.

I am proposing the numerical limitation of all immigration. Let the maximum annual male immigration from any particular people be some definite per cent (say five) of the sum of the American-born children of that people plus the naturalized citizens of the same people.

4. Those who are admitted **should be aided in the process of Americanization.**

5. And when they have reached the required standards of citizenship they should be naturalized. **Qualification for citizenship should be personal. All who qualify should be naturalized, regardless of race.**

Would not such a policy as this meet the appeal of Asia to the people of America, and yet do it in such a way as to safeguard all the real interests of our Pacific Coast States?

If, however, the problems of Asia arising from the white man's aggressions are to be fully met, we must do much more than has been thus far suggested.

Steps must be found for inducing the nations to return to China what has been taken from her: Hong Kong, Shanghai, Port Arthur, Kiao-Chao, Wei-hai-wei, Kwanchau. As the decades pass, these foreign-owned ports will become increasing causes of national resentment and indignation.

If China can be given justice by the great nations of the world without being compelled to do so at the point of Chinese bayonets, the great war between the East and West will be averted. If the West forces China into aggressive militarism in order to secure safety and justice, the future of the world is indeed ominous.

Does not the United States have a splendid opportunity for leading the nations into a right attitude toward Japan and China? How can she meet her responsibility and respond to that opportunity unless she first provides for justice in her own relations with Asia?

18

IMPORTANT BOOKS
BY
PROF. SIDNEY L. GULICK, M.A., D.D.

America and the Orient

Outlines of A Constructive Policy. Missionary Education Movement, pp. 100, N. Y.—1916—25c.

This little volume is an entirely fresh discussion of the whole problem of the race contact of the East and the West and the needed policy for the wholesome control of that contact. The author considers with care and criticizes in detail the two most widely advocated policies namely, "White Race World Supremacy" and "World Segregation of the White and Yellow Races." He asks what effects each of these policies would inevitably have on the two races themselves and on their mutual relations. Having shown the inevitable disasters, economic, political and international, that would follow from the full adoption of either of these policies, the author proceeds to develop the third policy which he names "The New Internationalism." This involves Federal legislation for dealing with Asiatics in the United States and a new diplomacy that concerns itself with the rights and welfare of Oriental peoples no less than with those of the United States. The appendix gives important statistics and charts illustrating the author's proposals regarding restriction of all immigration on a percentage basis and also a full and well classified bibliography of books and magazine articles dealing with American Asiatic questions.

The American-Japanese Problem

A Study of the Racial Relations of the East and West. Charles Scribner Sons, N. Y. 1914. $1.75.

A clear, impressive, and illuminating account of the situation in regard to the Japanese in California, and a thorough, scientific discussion of the possibilities of the Japanese, in this country as immigrants and citizens. Dr. Gulick shows by illustration and argument the reasonable, honorable, and satisfactory solution of a difficult question. In a very interesting and entertaining way he discusses every side of the question, both from the Japanese and American point of view, and his conclusions, in regard to past events and future possibilities, are most valuable and important.

IMPORTANT BOOKS

BY

PROF. SIDNEY L. GULICK, M.A., D.D.

Evolution of the Japanese Social and Psychic

8 vo., fifth edition, 1905. $2.00. Revell Co., N. Y.

The late *Prof. William James*—"I cannot withhold the tribute of my admiration. It makes me understand the Japanese as I never did before. It is a real pleasure to find a book that holds from beginning to end to psychological principles and to the realities of human nature. . . . A genuine work of interpretation and a model for future studies in ethnic character."

The Fight for Peace

An Aggressive Campaign for American Churches. Federal Council, 105 East 22nd St., N. Y.—1915— pp. 190—50c.

Rev. Francis E. Clark, D.D.—"There are few among the many books upon the peace question which I have read in these war times that seem to me so important and timely as Dr. Sidney Gulick's. I can heartily endorse his position in every particular. It seems to me that we must look more and more, not to the diplomats and statesmen, large as will be their influence in defining the terms and methods of a permanent peace, but to the Christians of America. These we can reach only through the organizations of the churches on a large scale for this purpose."

TWO PAMPHLETS AND A LEAFLET

Asia's Appeal to America and
A Comprehensive Immigration Policy and Program

The first pamphlet describes the serious international problem, due to America's disregard of treaty relations and differential race legislation, while the second pamphlet presents the method of solution that Dr. Gulick has been urging. Five cents each or $4.00 per hundred.

America's Asiatic Problem and Its Solution in a Nutshell is a six page leaflet which attempts to present in the briefest possible space both the problem and the proposed solution. Sixty cents per hundred, $5.00 per thousand.

www.ingramcontent.com/pod-product-compliance
Lightning Source LLC
Chambersburg PA
CBHW051349290326
41933CB00042B/3351